Sea

by the same author

IN A GREEN NIGHT: POEMS 1948–60
SELECTED POEMS
THE CASTAWAY
THE GULF AND OTHER POEMS
DREAM ON MONKEY MOUNTAIN AND OTHER PLAYS
ANOTHER LIFE

DEREK WALCOTT

Sea Grapes

JONATHAN CAPE
THIRTY BEDFORD SQUARE LONDON

FIRST PUBLISHED IN 1976
© 1976 BY DEREK WALCOTT
JONATHAN CAPE LTD, 30 BEDFORD SQUARE, LONDON WCI
ISBN 0 224 01231 2

Condition of Sale

This book is sold subject to the condition that it shall not, by way of trade or otherwise, be lent, re-sold, hired out, or otherwise circulated without the publisher's prior consent, in any form of binding or cover other than that in which it is published and without a similar condition including this condition being imposed on the subsequent purchaser.

SET IN 11PT IBM BASKERVILLE TWO PTS LEADED
PRINTED PHOTOLITHO IN GREAT BRITAIN
BY EBENEZER BAYLIS AND SON LIMITED,
THE TRINITY PRESS, WORCESTER, AND LONDON

to Margaret

Acknowledgments

Tapia (Trinidad), *New Letters* (Kansas City), *Chicago Tribune*, *London Magazine*, *Co-operation* (Canada), *Guyana Festival Anthology*, *Antaeus*. The poems entitled 'To Return to the Trees' and 'Sunday Lemons', 'The Bright Field' and 'Midsummer England' appeared originally in the *New Yorker*; © 1974, 1974, 1976, 1976, The New Yorker Magazine, Inc.

Contents

Sea Grapes	9
The Virgins	10
Frederiksted Nights	11
Frederiksted, Dusk	13
Sunday Lemons	14
Schloss Erla	16
The Cloud	17
New World	18
Adam's Song	20
Vigil in the Desert	22
The Brother	23
Preparing For Exile	25
Party Night at the Hilton	26
The Lost Federation	27
Parades, Parades	29
The Silent Woman	31
Dread Song	32
The Dream	35
Natural History	36
Names	40
Sainte Lucie	43
Over Colorado	56
Spring Street in '58	57
Ohio, Winter	59
For Pablo Neruda	60
Volcano	62
The Wind in the Dooryard	64
The Chelsea	67
The Bridge	69

Endings	71
California	72
The Fist	73
Love After Love	74
Midsummer, England	75
The Bright Field	77
Dark August	79
Sea Canes	81
The Harvest	82
Midsummer, Tobago	83
Force	84
Oddjob, a Bull Terrier	85
Earth	87
At Last	88
Winding Up	91
The Morning Moon	92
To Return to the Trees	93

Sea Grapes

That little sail in light
which tires of islands,
a schooner beating up the Caribbean

for home, could be Odysseus,
home-bound on the Aegean,
that father and husband's

longing, under gnarled sour grapes, is
like the adulterer hearing Nausicaa's name
in every gull's outcry;

This brings nobody peace. The ancient war
between obsession and responsibility
will never finish and has been the same

for the sea-wanderer or the one on shore
now wriggling on his sandals to walk home,
since Troy lost its old flame,

and the blind giant's boulder heaved the trough
from whose ground-swell the great hexameters come
to finish up as Caribbean surf.

The classics can console. But not enough.

The Virgins

Down the dead streets of sun-stoned Frederiksted,
the first freeport to die for tourism,
strolling at funeral pace, I am reminded
of life not lost to the American dream,
but my small-islander's simplicities,
can't better our new empire's civilized
exchange of cameras, watches, perfumes, brandies
for the good life, so cheaply underpriced
that only the crime rate is on the rise
in streets blighted with sun, stone arches
and plazas blown dry by the hysteria
of rumour. A condominium drowns
in vacancy; its bargains are dusted,
but only a jewelled housefly drones
over the bargains. The roulettes spin
rustily to the wind; the vigorous trade
that every morning would begin afresh
by revving up green water round the pierhead
heading for where the banks of silver thresh.

Frederiksted Nights

The goombay band or whatever
combination of Chicano charge
and black funk ignites the fish-fries
by the sizzling pierhead
with the sharks of submarines cruising
like the Puerta Ricenan putas
or lemon Dominican whores
the electric guitars rocketing
at the terrified, empty hotels,
all anger in the groin,
the bomb-cock,
the crotch-trap,
the thudding, explosive pelvis,
to which even the yachts nod,
to which a volley of bullets
sputters under the coalpots,
are gone dead
short-circuited.
The moon is a blown bulb.

And the La Cuenca Café
which only means 'The Corner'
a beastly green, pink and beige
is also out. Closed.
The plastic tablecloths are whipped away,
the defeated Chicano proprietor
gone back to the Main, maybe.
What is remarkable is
that he has taken you with him,

when he served us,
I did not know you would be stolen,
There is nothing around La Cuenca.

There is only the white street,
with the white gates and the oleanders,
and a library full of dead books,
houses, the ochre poorhouse, a hotel,
banks. It is simply another town.
It is simply fish-fry music,
or so I tell myself. Simply.

But my eyes wince at the names of shops
the empty tables are eating my heart;
nothing shines,
your radiance also turned off
by your own hand. So, tonight
when the foolish moon
gapes at the stupid pier,
and the boring music blares

I'll kick its ashes with my foot,
the fishbones, the cold songs,
feel vague as the moon in daylight,
and abhor the cheap green curtains
of the La Cuenca Café.

My life has no corners to turn.
You are young. Go.
I will not turn down any more alleys
to find someone as astonishing;
and in the end, one always
comes to this,
to the dock,
the rain-hazed horizon
and the corpses of poems.

Frederiksted, Dusk

Sunset, the cheapest of all picture-shows,
was all they waited for: old men like empties
set down from morning outside the alms-house,
to let the rising evening brim their eyes,
and, in one row, return the level stare
of light that shares its mortal properties
with the least stone in Frederiksted, as if
more than mortality brightened the air,
like a girl tanning on a rock alone
who fills with light. Whatever it is
that leaves bright flesh like sand and turns it chill,
not age alone, they were old, but a state
made possible by their collective will,
would shine in them like something between life
and death, our two concrete simplicities,
and waited too in, seeming not to wait,
substantial light and insubstantial stone.

Sunday Lemons

Desolate lemons, hold
tight, in your bowl of earth,
the light to your bitter flesh,

let a lemon glare
be all your armour
this naked Sunday,

your inflexible light
bounce off the shields of apples
so real, they seem waxen,

share your acid silence
with this woman's remembering
Sundays of other fruit,

till by concentration
you grow, a phalanx of helmets
braced for anything,

hexagonal cities where bees
died purely for sweetness,
your lamps be the last to go

on this polished table
this Sunday, which demands
more than the faith of candles

than helmeted conquistadors

dying like bees, multiplying
memories in her golden head;

as the afternoon vagues
into indigo, let your lamps
hold in this darkening earth

bowl, still life, but a life
beyond tears or the gaieties
of dew, the gay, neon damp

of the evening that blurs
the form of this woman lying,
a lemon, a flameless lamp.

Schloss Erla

Summer lies drugged with prose,
beer-bellied, like Brueghel,
bee-droned. The folk drowse
by the dragonfly-stung pool
where ring on hypnotic ring
widens. The rings will settle,
the air change, and quietly, a chill
flute give every leaf a fatal
edge. Prepare the fall; the fall,
when apples find the subtleties
of autumn sweetest. On the wall
of your New York apartment
you have hung a small summer
picture of Schloss Erla. You fill
and ring your reverie with smoke
around fire-coloured hair.
It is August in Austria.
Castles are lost to a horizon
frail as ash, as far
away as wood-smoke. The zone
that is your sadness rings you,
but sadness is your season
like the apples, as you ripen
to a fullness that can endure
the blazing lie of summer; for,
at the core of passion, you've
always sensed the cold.

The Cloud

And, laterally,
to Adam's pulsing eye,
the erect ridges would throb and recede,

a sigh under the fig tree and a sky
deflating to the serpent's punctured hiss,
repeating you will die.

The woman lay still as the settling mountains.
There was another silence
all was thick with it;

the clouds given a mortal destination,
the silent shudder from the broken branch
where the sap dripped

from the torn tree.
When she, his death,
turned on her side and slept,
the breath he drew was his first real breath.

What left the leaves,
the phosphorescent air
was both God and the serpent leaving him.
Neither could curse or bless.

Pollen was drifting to the woman's hair,
his eye felt brighter,
a cloud's slow shadow slowly covered them,

and, as it moved, he named it Tenderness.

New World

Then after Eden,
was there one surprise?
O yes, the awe of Adam
at the first bead of sweat.

Thenceforth, all flesh
had to be sown with salt,
to feel the edge of seasons,
fear and harvest,
joy, that was difficult,
but was, at least, his own.

The snake? It would not rust
on its forked tree.
The snake admired labour,
it would not leave him alone.

And both would watch the leaves
silver the alder,
oaks yellowing October,
everything turning money,

so when Adam was exiled
to our New Eden, in the ark's gut,
the coined snake coiled there for good
fellowship also; that was willed.

Adam had an idea.
He and the snake would share
the loss of Eden for a profit.
So both made the New World. And it looked good.

Adam's Song

The adulteress stoned to death,
is killed in our own time
by whispers, by the breath
that films her flesh with slime.

The first was Eve,
who horned God for the serpent,
for Adam's sake; which makes
everyone guilty or Eve innocent.

Nothing has changed
for men still sing the song that Adam sang
against the world he lost to vipers,

the song to Eve
against his own damnation;
he sang it in the evening of the world

with the lights coming on in the eyes
of panthers in the peaceable kingdom
and his death coming out of the trees,

he sings it, frightened
of the jealousy of God and at the price
of his own death,

the song ascends to God who wipes his eyes

'Heart, you are in my heart as the bird rises,
heart, you are in my heart while the sun sleeps,
heart, you lie still in me as the dew is,
you weep within me, as the rain weeps.'

Vigil in the Desert

It is from our friends, the hyenas,
with rotting laughter
that, maimed, we have come to choose
the desert dignities of silence,

the dry peace of the anchorite
that whips their parched throats to bark:
barren! Barren!

While, by this runnel
of ferns, we hoard
every syllabic raindrop

where the sky bends
like a bay window
that holds the tiny jewelled head of God

who multiplies in every bead
while round and round and round
the gritted smile of the hermit

circle the evangelical hyenas.

The Brother

That smiler next to you who whispers
brother

knife him.

That man who borrowed your coat
the one of many colours

reclaim it as yours.

Fear your best friends like fire,
it's the cost of this winter,

take him again into your heart's cave

but bind him.

That crippled angel, the Bactrian
who eased your arse out of your own tent,
maim him;

they know when you imitate Christ,
but no man has three cheeks,
and treachery exhausts the patience

even of false saints.
Move from the breath that is soured by envy,
move from those who never have change
but exact thirty pieces of silver

in the name of a cause.
They light a flare in the brain
that cannot let you rest.

And when your love is spent,
in Eden, who sleeps happiest?
The serpent.

Preparing for Exile

Why do I imagine the death of Mandelstam
among the yellowing coconuts,
why does my gift already look over its shoulder
for a shadow to fill the door
and pass this very page into eclipse?
Why does the moon increase into an arc-lamp
and the inkstain on my hand prepare to press thumb-downward
before a shrugging sergeant?
What is this new odour in the air
that was once salt, that smelt like lime at daybreak,
and my cat, I know I imagine it, leap from my path,
and my children's eyes already seem like horizons,
and all my poems, even this one, wish to hide?

Party Night at the Hilton

In our upside-down hotel, in that air-conditioned
roomful of venal, vengeful party-hacks,
lunch-drunk, scotch-drunk, cigar and brandy-stoned,
arguing, insulting till coherence cracks,
poor voice on the rock of power, drained
of every sense but retching indignation
before these pimp Nkrumahs! Their minds
greased by infanticide, generation on generation
heaped in a famine of imagination,
while dacrons sleek their paunches and behinds
with air, hot air. Guilt, sweated
out in glut, while outside, a black wind,
circles the room with jasmine, like a whore's
perfume or second secretary's lotion. Fear those laws
which ex-slaves praise with passion. Pissed, dead
drunk, I soar to hellish light. In the lobby,
cigars with eyes like agents drilling me.

The Lost Federation

You should crawl into rocks away from
the stare of the fisherman,
you, yes, you!

Don't you remember the hustings by the beach
with their sulphurous lanterns,
and your lies in the throat of the sea?

You should get your arse baked till your back
is an old map of blisters,
and your lips crack

like the soil for the water you promised
on the dais, with the sound system
and the sisters calling you Jesus,

and come back with a sieve for your heart,
your brain like a rusted can,
and your bilge reeking,

turn your head, man, I'm speaking
now, I haven't spoken enough, I am speaking
so do what you want, man!

When the first roar came you were astounded,
it was sweeping your heart like a hurricane;
but what are your promises? A grounded

ribbed vessel that the naked
children play through. Listen, you

could still come with me again,
to watch the rain coming from far
like rain, not like votes,

like the ocean, like the wind,
not like an overwhelming majority,
you, who served the people a dung cake of maggots,

that rain cannot extinguish
the processional flambeaux of the poui,
the immortelles, feel it with me

again, you bastard papas,
how it seeps through the pores,
how it loads the sponge of the heart

with the grief of a people,
or smile at this rage, then,
buzzard in a conference coat,

bishop in buzzard's surplice,
crows circling like shadows
over this page,

ministers administering
the last rights to a people,
cabinet, crowded with skeletons,

here's a swinging convocation of bishops
and ministers on the old beach.
Corbeaux. And nobody here with a flashbulb!

Parades, Parades

There's the wide desert, but no one marches
except in the pads of old caravans,
there is the ocean, but the keels incise
the precise, old parallels,
there's the blue sea above the mountains
but they scratch the same lines
in the jet trails,
so the politicians plod
without imagination, circling
the same sombre gardens
with its fountain dry in the forecourt,
the gri-gri palms desicating
dung pods like goats,
the same lines rule the White Papers,
the same steps ascend Whitehall,
and only the name of the fool changes
under the plumed white cork-hat
for the Independence Parades
revolving around, in calypso,
to the brazen joy of the tubas.

Why are the eyes of the beautiful
and unmarked children
in the uniforms of the country
bewildered and shy,
why do they widen in terror
of the pride drummed into their minds?
Were they truer, the old songs,
when the law lived far away,

when the veiled queen, her girth
as comfortable as cushions,
upheld the orb with its stern admonitions?
We wait for the changing of statues,
for the change of parades.

Here he comes now, here he comes!
Papa! Papa! With his crowd,
the sleek, waddling seals of his Cabinet,
trundling up to the dais,
as the wind puts its tail between
the cleft of the mountain, and a wave
coughs once, abruptly.
Who will name this silence
respect? Those forced, hoarse hosannas
awe? That tin-ringing tune
from the pumping, circling horns
the New World? Find a name
for that look on the faces
of the electorate. Tell me
how it all happened, and why
I said nothing.

The Silent Woman

for Jean Miles

'No, not under the vault of another sky,
not under the shelter of other wings.
I was with my people then,
there where my people were doomed to be.'

Anna Akhmatova

Now the executives in business suits,
the dealers in shrugs and smiles
like all the other smilers who have lived
can settle with relief now
to their luncheons, appointments and commissions,
because her final silence has arrived,
until another like her, some woman
or man with the heart of this woman,
some accounts clerk, some public servant, broken
again, by the cost in agony
of public service, speaks. Miss Miles,
it was better to be broken
than like the rest, your betters,
to leave the truth, unspoken.
Come gentlemen, you aren't that busy, come Creon,
come, help Antigone lift up this woman.

Dread Song

Forged from the fire of Exodus
the iron of the tribe,

bright as the lion light, Isaiah,
the anger of the tribe

that the crack must come
and sunder the stone

and the sky-stone fall
on Babylon, Babylon,

the crack in the prison wall
in the chasm of tenements

when the high, high C, Joshua
cry, as I for my tribe:

but in the black markets
lizard-smart poets

selling copper tributes
changing skin with the tribe

and the tribe still buys it
the dreams and the lies

that there'll come to market
as the brethren divide

like the Red Sea to Moses
halt by Aaron's rod

the rod which is both serpent
and staff of brotherhood

more cripples like questions
on the snakes of black tires

Solomon in black glasses
hiding his eyes

shaking hands all round
statistics and jiving

to the clapping of the tribe;
Economics and Exodus,

embrace us within
bracket and parenthesis

their snake arms of brotherhood
(the brackets of the bribe)

Want to open your mouth, then?
Shake your dread locks, brethren?

and see one door yawn wide,
then the lion-den of prison,

sky mortar like stone;
Brothers in Babylon, Doc! Uncle! Papa!

Behind the dark glasses
the fire is dying

the coal of my people;
no vision, no flame,

no deepness, no danger,
more music, less anger

more sorrow, less shame
more talk of the River

that wash out my name
let things be the same

forever and ever
the faith of my tribe.

The Dream

I stood on the sand, I saw
black horsemen galloping towards
me, they were all white like
the waves and turbanned too
like the breakers, their flags
thinning away into spume; white,
white were their snorting horses.
I saw them. It was no dream. They
rode through me, they came from
my home, as fresh as the waves
and older than this sea.
Rider and breaker, one cry!
I have seen them at a ceremony
of lances, white-robed knights,
(I forget the names of our tribes).
They are coming, I trembled, to claim
their brothers, to bring them
home, thundering round the edge
of the headland, exploding from sight!
Spears shoot on the edge
of the wave every moonlit night —
The horsemen will keep their pledge,
the knights of Bornu.

Natural History
I
The Walking Fish

There was a shape across the bay,
stunned on the sand.
It was like a huge fish, or a man
like a huge fish.

It did not move. I could not look away.
It was here I began.
The waves

scudded over my back;
where they snagged they formed scales
scalloped at the edges. My ducts
subside now. Bellows.

For years
my sky has been water;
I have paddled under the bubbles
of phosphorescent moons,

my eyes
glazed by a film
that set into gelatinous scales,
their quick salt itch drying.

The scallops
harden, the nostrils shrivel,
splayed, the webbed fingers burrow
into this sand.

I'll wait.
Waves, waves wash over my back.
The tears prickle quickly out of my eye.

I'll wait
for a geological epoch
My biggest thrill is a blink
One blink every geological epoch.

The waves now
have receded into the far, faint
caves of my ears. I shed glazed
fins like sea-fans, dragon-serrated.

This beach,
is just like the other where I was born.
I feel green and black with a chain-mail
of silver, then a fine net of pores

through which the sea breathes
through which the Atlantic remembers,
through which in flutes the five oceans whistle

Lumber once, then
stop. Dragons no longer fly,
the groaning mastodon's gone down

in the brea of muck
the tiger's sabres turned coral,
the pterodactyl shrunk to a bat,

but I name
this foothold with a grateful croak,
earth. I can arch my back

I can squat,

I can paddle my forefins,
fingers of grass in the sand
and grass in my fingers

Lurch up.
Earth falls away. Up.
The horizon drops past my belly.

Dunes, there,
behind the dunes, others,
my kind, other gutturals waiting,

learning
their unsteady walk.
There is nothing in that ocean
above the horizon,

in that sea,
where the great white fish swam,
everything has changed

or has changed us.
Or, as I
paddle this air, breathe this new sea, am I
still swimming through one gigantic eye?

II
Frogs

Moonlight, and the sun-dials of frogs sadden the lawn.
Tires will grind them like head-lamp marbled crabs, like splayed
Biafran children, and tomorrow's sun
reprint them till they take on
the monochrome of asphalt
the tabloid, iron tones of death. History

is natural; famine, genocide,
as natural as moonlight,
and man is great who rises at this cost;
like the Bikini turtles, who, after the holocaust
swam deeper into sand, their history reversed
from nature, or the mad birds
that burrowed into earth, while ocean,
a god once, rages, at a loss for words.

III
Turtles

To have misplaced your instinct for the sea,
to blunder with each cataracted eye
staring past panic, or panic so bland,
the gripping, slipping paddles row through sand
changed by man's will to ocean.
The mutant turtles teach adaptability
to man, the walking fish,
who with his forefins used to pray upright,
before the bomb's fountaining: 'Let there be light!'

IV
Butterflies

They fall in ribbons down the paths of ocean,
the foam-pale butterflies, but the flowers are salt.
They prove the charms of rapine, that the emotion
called beauty has earned this result.

Names

for Edward Brathwaite

I

My race began as the sea began,
with no nouns, and with no horizon,
with pebbles under my tongue,
with a different fix on the stars.

But now my race is here,
in the sad oil of Levantine eyes,
in the flags of the Indian fields,

I began with no memory,
I began with no future,
but I looked for that moment
when the mind was halved by a horizon,

I have never found that moment
when the mind was halved by a horizon
for the goldsmith from Benares,
the stone-cutter from Canton,
as a fishline sinks, the horizon
sinks in the memory.

Have we melted into a mirror,
leaving our souls behind?
The goldsmith from Benares,
the stone-cutter from Canton,
the bronzesmith from Benin.

A sea-eagle screams from the rock,
and my race began like the osprey

with that cry,
that terrible vowel,
that I!

Behind us all the sky folded,
as history folds over a fishline,
and the foam foreclosed
with nothing in our hands

but this stick
to trace our names on the sand
which the sea erased again, to our indifference.

II

And when they named these bays
bays,
was it nostalgia or irony?

In the uncombed forest,
in uncultivated grass
where was there elegance
except in their mockery?
Where were the courts of Castille,
Versailles' colonnades
supplanted by cabbage palms
with Corinthian crests,
belittling diminutives,
then, little Versailles
meant plans for a pigsty,
names for the sour apples
and green grapes
of their exile.

Their memory turned acid
but the names held,
Valencia glows
with the lanterns of oranges,
Mayaro's
charred candelabra of cocoa.
Being men, they could not live
except they first presumed
the right of every thing to be a noun.
The African acquiesced,
repeated, and changed them

Listen, my children, say:
moubain: the hogplum,
cerise: the wild cherry,
baie-la: the bay,
with the fresh green voices
they were once themselves
in the way the wind bends
our natural inflections.

These palms are greater than Versailles,
for no man made them,
their fallen columns greater than Castille,
no man unmade them
except the worm, who has no helmet,
but was always the emperor,

and children, look at these stars
over Valencia's forest!

Not Orion,
not Betelgeuse,
tell me, what do they look like?
Answer, you damned little Arabs!
Sir, fireflies caught in molasses.

Sainte Lucie

I
The Villages

Laborie, Choiseul, Vieuxfort, Dennery,
from these sun-bleached villages
where the church-bell caves in the sides
of one grey-scurfed shack that is shuttered
with warped boards, with rust
with crabs crawling under the house-shadow
where the children played house;
a net rotting among cans, the sea-net
of sunlight trolling the shallows
catching nothing all afternoon,
from these I am growing no nearer
to what secret eluded the children
under the house-shade, in the far bell, the noon's
stunned amethystine sea,
something always being missed
between the floating shadow and the pelican
in the smoke from over the next bay
in that shack on the lip of the sandpit
whatever the seagulls cried out for
with the grey drifting ladders of rain
and the great grey tree of the waterspout,
for which the dolphins kept diving, that
should have rounded the day.

II

Pomme arac,
otaheite apple,
pomme cythere,

pomme granate,
moubain,
z'anananas
the pine apple's
Aztec helmet,
pomme,
I have forgotten
what pomme for
the Irish potato,
cerise,
the cherry,
z'aman
sea-almonds
by the crisp
sea-bursts,
au bord de la 'ouviere.
Come back to me
my language.
Come back,
cacao,
grigri,
solitaire,
ciseau
the scissor-bird
no nightingales
except, once,
in the indigo mountains
of Jamaica, blue depth,
deep as coffee,
flicker of pimento,
the shaft light
on a yellow ackee
the bark alone bare

jardins
en montagnes

en haut betassion
the wet leather reek
of the hill donkey

evening opens at
a text of fireflies,
in the mountain huts
ti cailles betassion
candles,
candleflies
the black night bending
cups in its hard palms
cool thin water
this is important water,
important?
imported?
water is important
also very important
the red rust drum
the evening deep
as coffee
the morning powerful
important coffee
the villages shut
all day in the sun.

In the empty schoolyard
teacher dead today
the fruit rotting
yellow on the ground,
dyes from Gauguin
the pomme arac dyes
the earth purple,
the ochre roads
still waiting in the sun
for my shadow,

O so you is Walcott?
you is Roddy brother?
Teacher Alix son?
and the small rivers
with important names.

And the important corporal
in the country station
en betassion
looking towards the thick
green slopes of cocoa
the sun that melts
the asphalt at noon,
and the woman in the shade
of the breadfruit bent over
the lip of the valley,
below her, blue-green
the lost, lost valleys
of sugar, the bus-rides,
the fields of bananas
the tanker still rusts
in the lagoon at Roseau,
and around what corner

was uttered a single
yellow leaf,
from the frangipani
a tough bark, reticent,
but when it flowers
delivers hard lilies,
pungent, recalling
Martina, or Eunice
or Lucilla,
who comes down the steps
with the cool, side flow
as spring water eases

over shelves of rock
in some green ferny hole
by the road in the mountains,
her smile like the whole country
her smell, earth,
red-brown earth, her armpits
a reaping, her arms
saplings, an old woman
that she is now,
with other generations
of daughters flowing
down the steps,
gens betassion,
belle ti fille betassion,
until their teeth go,
and all the rest,

O Martinas, Lucillas,
I'm a wild golden apple
that will burst with love,
of you and your men,
those I never told enough
with my young poet's eyes
crazy with the country,
generations going,
generations gone,
moi c'est gens St Lucie.
C'est la moi sorti;
is there that I born.

III
Iona: Mabouya Valley

(Saint Lucian *conte* or narrative song, heard on the back
of an open truck travelling to Vieuxfort, some years ago)

Ma Kilman, Bon Dieu kai punir 'ous,
Pour qui raison parcequi' ous entrer trop religion.
Oui, l'autre cote, Bon Dieu kai benir 'ous,
Bon Dieu kai benir 'ous parcequi 'ous faire charite l'argent.
Corbeau aille Curacao, i' voyait l'argent ba 'ous,
Ous prend l'argent cela
Ous mettait lui en cabaret.
Ous pas ka lire, ecrire, 'ous pas ka parler Anglais,
Ous tait supposer ca; cabaret pas ni benefice.
L'heure Corbeau devirait,
L'tait ni, I' tait ni l'argent,
L'heure i' rivait ici,
Oui, maman! Corbeau kai fou!

Iona dit Corbeau, pendant 'ous tait Curacao,
Moi fait deux 'tits mamaille, venir garder si c'est ca 'ous,
Corbeau criait 'Mama! Bon soir, messieurs, mesdames,
Lumer lampe-la ba mwen
Pour moi garder ces mamailles-la!'
Corbeau virait dire: 'Moi save toutes negres ka semble,
I peut si pas ca moin,
Moi kai soigner ces mamailles-la!'

Oui, Corbeau partit, Corbeau descend Roseau,
Allait chercher travail, pourqui 'peut soigner ces mamailles-la,
Iona dit Corbeau pas tait descendre Roseau,
Mais i' descend Roseau, jamettes Rosseau tomber derriere-i'

Phillipe Mago achetait un sax bai Corbeau,
I' pas ni temps jouer sax-la,
Sax-man comme lui prendre la vie-lui.

Samedi bon matin, Corbeau partit descendre en ville,
Samedi apres-midi, nous 'tendre la mort Corbeau.
Ca fait moi la peine; oui, ca brulait coeur-moin,
Ca penetrait moin, l'heure moin 'tendre la mort Corbeau.

Iona dit comme-ca: ca qui fait lui la peine,
Ca qui brulait coeur-lui: saxophone Corbeau pas jouer.
Moin 'tendre un corne cornait
a sur bord roseaux-a,
Moi dit: 'Doux-doux, moin kai chercher volants ba 'ous'
L'heure moin 'rivait la, moin fait raconte epi Corbeau,
I' dit: 'Corne-la qui cornait-a,
c'est Iona ka cornait moin.'

Guitar-man la ka dire:
'Nous tous les deux c'est guitar-man,
Pas prendre ca pour un rien,
C'est meme beat-la nous ka chember.'

Iona mariee, Dimanche a quatre heures.
Mardi, a huit heures, i' aille l'hopital.
I'fait un bombe, mari-lui cassait bras-lui.
L'heure moi joindre maman-ous,
Moin kai conter toute ca 'ous 'ja faire moin.
Iona!
(N'ai dit maman-ous!)
Iona!
(Ous pas ka 'couter moin!)
Trois jours, trois nuits
Iona bouillit, Iona pas chuitte.
(N'ai dit maman-i' ca)
Toute moune ka dit Iona tourner,

C'est pas tourner Iona tourner, mauvais i' mauvais,
Iona!

IV
Iona: Mabouya Valley
for Eric Branford

Ma Kilman God will punish you,
for the reason that you've got too much religion,
on the other hand, God will bless you,
God will bless you because of your charity.

Corbeau went to Curacao
He sent you money back
You took the same money
and put it in a rum-shop
You can't read, you can't write, you can't speak English,
You should know that rum-shops make no profit,
When Corbeau come back
He had, yes he had money
when he arrived back here,
Yes Mama, Corbeau'll go crazy.

Iona told Corbeau while you were in Curacao
I made two little children, come and see if they're yours.
Corbeau cried out, 'Mama, Goodnight ladies and gentlemen
Light the lamp there for me
For me to look at these kids,'
Corbeau came back and said 'I know niggers resemble,
They may or may not be mine,
I'll mind them all the same.'

Ah yes, Corbeau then left, he went down to Roseau,

He went to look for work, to mind the two little ones,
Iona told Corbeau, don't go down to Roseau
But he went to Roseau, and Roseau's whores fell on him.
Phillipe Mago, brought Corbeau a saxophone,
He had no time to play the sax
A saxman just like him took away his living.

Saturday morning early, Corbeau goes into town.
Saturday afternoon we hear Corbeau is dead.
That really made me sad, that really burnt my heart;
That really went through me when I heard Corbeau was dead.

Iona said like this: it made her sorry too,
It really burnt her heart, that the saxophone will never play.

I heard a horn blowing
by the river reeds down there
Sweetheart, I said, I'll go looking
for flying fish for you.
When I got there, I came across Corbeau
He said that horn you heard
was Iona horning me.

The guitar man's saying
We both are guitar men,
Don't take it for anything,
We both holding the same beat.

Iona got married, Sunday at four o'clock.
Tuesday, by eight o'clock, she's in the hospital.
She made a fare, her husband broke her arm,
when I meet your mother I'll tell what you did me.
Iona,
(I'll tell your maman)
Iona
(You don't listen to me)

Three days and three nights
(Iona boiled, she's still not cooked)
(I'll tell her mother that)
They say Iona's changed
It isn't changed Iona's changed
she's wicked, wicked, that's all
Iona.

V
For the Altar-piece of the Roseau Valley Church, Saint Lucia

I

The chapel, as the pivot of this valley,
round which whatever is rooted loosely turns
men, women, ditches, the revolving fields
of bananas, the secondary roads,
draws all to it, to the altar
and the massive altar-piece;
like a dull mirror, life
repeated there,
the common life outside
and the other life it holds
a good man made it.

Two earth-brown labourers
dance the botay in it, the drum sounds under
the earth, the heavy foot.

                              This is a rich valley,
   It is fat with things.

Its roads radiate like aisles from the altar towards
those acres of bananas, towards
leaf-crowded mountains
rain-bellied clouds
in haze, in iron heat;

                     This is a cursed valley,
ask the broken mules, the swollen children,
ask the dried women, their gap-toothed men,
ask the parish priest, who, in the altar-piece
carries a replica of the church,
ask the two who could be Eve and Adam dancing.

II

Five centuries ago
in the time of Giotto
this altar might have had
in one corner, when God was young
ST OMER ME FECIT AETAT whatever his own age now,
GLORIA DEI and to God's Mother also.

It is signed with music.
It turns the whole island.
You have to imagine it empty on a Sunday afternoon
between adorations

Nobody can see it and it is there,
nobody adores the two who could be Eve and Adam dancing.

A Sunday at three o'clock
when the real Adam and Eve have coupled
and lie in re-christening sweat

his sweat on her still breasts,
her sweat on his panelled torso

that hefts bananas
that has killed snakes
that has climbed out of rivers,

now, as on the furred tops of the hills
a breeze moving the hairs on his chest

on a Sunday at three o'clock
when the snake pours itself
into a chalice of leaves.

The sugar factory is empty.

Nobody picks bananas,
no trucks raising dust on their way to Vieuxfort,
no helicopter spraying

the mosquito's banjo, yes,
and the gnat's violin, okay,

okay, not absolute Adamic silence,
the valley of Roseau is not the Garden of Eden,
and those who inhabit it, are not in heaven,

so there are little wires of music
some marron up in the hills, by AuxLyons,
some christening.

A boy banging a tin by the river,
with the river trying to sleep.
But nothing can break that silence,

which comes from the depth of the world,
from whatever one man believes he knows of God
and the suffering of his kind,

it comes from the wall of the altar-piece
ST OMER AD GLORIAM DEI FECIT
in whatever year of his suffering.

III

After so many bottles of white rum in a pile,
after the flight of so many little fishes
from the brush that is the finger of St Francis,

after the deaths
of as many names as you want,
Iona, Julian, Ti-Nomme, Cacao,
like the death of the cane-crop in Roseau Valley, St Lucia.

After five thousand novenas
and the idea of the Virgin
coming and going like a little lamp

after all that,
your faith like a canoe at evening coming in,
like a relative who is tired of America,
like a woman coming back to your house

that sang in the ropes of your wrist
when you lifted this up;
so that, from time to time, on Sundays

between adorations, one might see,
if one were there, and not there,
looking in at the windows

the real faces of angels.

Over Colorado

When Whitman's beard unrolled like the Pacific,
when he quit talking
to prophesy the great waggons

the dream began to lumber to delirium.
Once, flying over Colorado
its starved palomino mountains

I saw, like ants, a staggering file
of Indians enter a cloud's beard;
then the cloud broke on

a frozen brave, his fossil
a fern-print on the spine of rock,
his snow-soft whisper

Colorado, rust and white;
the snow his praise, the snow
his obliterator.

That was years ago,
in a jet crossing to Los Angeles,
I don't know why it comes now,

or why I see only this
through those democratic vistas
parting your leaves of grass.

Spring Street in '58

for Frank O'Hara

Dirt under the fingernails of the window-ledge,
in the rococo ceiling, grime
flowering like a street opera.
Ah candles, Con-Edison nights
in the packing-case district
of my little Italy,
ah, my blown-out,
fly-blown Bohemia!

There was dirt on the peach tan
of the girls of the gold Mid-West,
ou sont ces vierges?
Ah, Frank, elles sont
aux Spring Falls, Iowa,
Columbus, Tucson,
gone with coarse ponytails, gone
with autumnal reveries of Indian blankets,
birches, and the snow creek on the calendar
quivering its palomino hide
to the housefly; back
to the picket fences, Minnesota,
to the strict elms that predicted their return,
to the flowered headscarves and the supermarkets
with the Evergreen Reviews they cannot burn.

And the cheap cocktail bars
by which I homed,
their neon flickered like Mars,
then, we could still write 'The moon . . .'

nostalgia was halvah and nougat
and was out of fashion, like death;
and one caught style from others like a cold,
and I could look at Mimi washing her soiled feet
as life imitating Lautrec.

In Spring Street's dirty hermitage, where I
crouched over poems, and drawings, I
knew we'd all live as long as Hokusai.

Ohio, Winter

for James Wright

It's your country, Jim, and what
I imagine there may not exist:
summer grass clutching derailed freight
trains till they rust
and blacken like buffalo.
This winter is white as wheat
and width is its terror, you're
right; behind the clenched, white
barns all afternoon the night
hides with a knife; the road
grovels under a blizzard,
frost glazes the eyelid
of the windscreen, and every barn or
farm-light goes lonelier, lonelier.

For Pablo Neruda

I am not walking on sand,
but I feel I am walking on sand,
this poem is accompanying me on sand.
Fungus lacing the rock,
on the ribs, mould. Moss
feathering the mute roar
of the staved in throat
of the wreck, the crab gripping.

Why this loop of correspondences,
as your voice grows hoarser
than the chafed Pacific? Your voice
falling soundless as snow on
the petrified Andes, the snow
like feathers from the tilting
rudderless condors,
emissary in a black suit, who
walks among eagles, hand, whose
five knuckled peninsula
bars the heartbreaking ocean?

Hear the ambassador of velvet
open the felt-hinged door,
the black flag flaps toothless
over Isla Negra. You said
when others like me despaired:
climb the moss-throated stairs
to the crest of Macchu Picchu,
break your teeth like a pick on

the obdurate, mottled terraces,
wear the wind, soaked with rain
like a cloak, above absences,

and for us, in the New World,
our older world, you become
a benign, rigorous uncle,
and through you we fanned open
to others, to the sand-rasped
mutter of César Vallejo, to
the radiant, self-circling
sunstone of Octavio, men
who, unlike the Saxons, I am tempted
to call by their Christian names

we were all netted to one rock
by vines of iron, our livers
picked by corbeaux and condors
in the New World, in a new word
brotherhood, word which arrests
the crests of the snowblowing ocean
in its flash to a sea of sierras,
the round fish mouths of our children
the word *cantan*. All this
you have done for me. Gracias.

Volcano

Joyce was afraid of thunder,
but lions roared at his funeral
from the Zurich zoo.
Was it Zurich or Trieste?
No matter. These are legends, as much
as the death of Joyce is a legend,
or the strong rumour that Conrad
is dead, and that VICTORY is ironic,
On the edge of the night-horizon
from this beach house on the cliffs
there are now, till dawn,
two glares from the miles-out
at sea derricks; they are like
the glow of the cigar
and the glow of the volcano
at VICTORY'S end.
One could abandon writing
for the slow-burning signals
of the great, to be, instead
their ideal reader, ruminative,
voracious, making the love of masterpieces
superior to attempting
to repeat or outdo them,
and be the greatest reader in the world.
At least it requires awe,
which has been lost to our time,
so many people have seen everything,
so many people can predict,
so many refuse to enter the silence

of victory, the indolence
that burns at the core,
so many are no more than
erect ash, like the cigar,
so many take thunder for granted.
How common is the lightning,
how lost the leviathans
we no longer look for!
There were giants in those days.
In those days they made good cigars.
I must read more carefully.

The Wind in the Dooryard

for Eric Roach

I didn't want this poem to come
from the torn mouth,
I didn't want this poem to come
from his salt body,

but I will tell you what he celebrated:

He writes of the wall with spilling coralita
from the rim of the rich garden,
and the clean dirt yard
clean as the parlour table
with a yellow tree
an ackee, an almond
a pomegranate
in the clear vase of sunlight,

sometimes he put his finger
on the pulse of the wind,
when he heard the sea in the cedars.
He went swimming to Africa,
but he felt tired,
he chose that way
to reach his ancestors.

No, I did not want to write this,
but, doesn't the sunrise
force itself through the curtain
of the trembling eyelids?
When the cows are statues in the misting field

that sweats out the dew,
and the horse lifts its iron head
and the jaws of the sugar mules
ruminate and grind like the factory?

I did not want to hear it again,
the echo of broken windmills,
the mutter of the wild yams creeping
over the broken palings,
the noise of the moss
stitching the stone baracoons,

but the rain breaks
on the foreheads of the wild yams,
the dooryard opens the voice
of his rusty theme,
and the first quick drops of the drizzle
the libations to Shango
dry fast as sweat on the forehead
and our tears also.

The peasant reeks sweetly of bush,
he smells the same as his donkey
they smell of the high, high country
of clouds and stunted pine,
the man wipes his hand
that is large as a yam
and as crusty with dirt
across the tobacco-stained
paling stumps of his torn mouth,
he rinses with the mountain dew,
and he spits out pity.

I did not want it to come,
but sometimes, under the armpit
of the hot sky over the country

the wind smells of salt
and a certain breeze lifts
the sprigs of the coralita
as if, like us,
lifting our heads, at our happiest,
it too smells the freshness of life.

The Chelsea

I

Nothing, not the hotel's beige dankness, not
the neon-flickered drifts of dirty rain,
the marigolds' drying fire from their pot
above a dead fireplace, mean ruin
anymore to him. The mirror's reflexes
are nerveless and indifferent as he is
to fame and money. He will find success
in the lost art of failure, so he says
to the flawless girl framed in the mirror's tarnish.
She's more than the hotel's bronze plaque of greats
who hit the bottle or the street, grew rich
or famous. Their fame curls like layers of beige
paint, just as those mirrored flowers will die.
The clear-eyed girl letting cold tap-water
run on, watches herself watching him lie.

II

Between the darkening drapes of the hotel
We'd watch the lion-coloured twilight come
stalking up the sandstone, tall
bluff of the West Side Gymnasium,
the wide sky yawning as the tame light curled
around Manhattan, then felt the room fill
with a vague pity, as its objects furred
to indistinction, chair, bed, desk, turn soft
as drowsing lions. Love gives a selfish strength
if lonely lives, down the stale corridors,
still, as they turn the key, nod down the length

of their whole life at slowly-closing doors,
In other's hell we made our happiness.
Across the window furnished room and loft
lamplit their intimacies. Happier lives,
settled in ruts, and great for wanting less.

The Bridge

Good-evening, here is the news.
Tonight here, in Manhattan, on a bridge,
a matter that began

two years ago between this man
and the woman next to him, is ending.
And that concludes the news for tonight,

except the old news of the river's fairy light,
and the bridge lit up
like the postcards, the cliché views,

except that they have nothing to grip the bridge with,
and across the river all the offices are on
for safety, they are like over-typed carbon

held up to light with the tears showing.
The heart, that is girded iron melts. The iron
bridge is an empty party. A man a feather.

There are too many lights on.
It's far too fanciful; that's all;
the iron rainbow to the bright water bending.

Neither is capable of going
they stand like still beasts in a hunter's moon,
silent like beasts, but soon,

the woman
will sense in her eyes dawn's rain beginning,
and the man

feel in his muscles the river's startled flowing.

Endings

Things do not explode
they fail, they fade,

as sunlight fades from the flesh
as the foam drains quick in the sand,

even love's lightning flash
has no thunderous end,

it dies with the sound
of flowers fading like the flesh

from sweating pumice stone,
everything shapes this

till we are left
with the silence that surrounds Beethoven's head.

California

Heal me, valley.
The gull
names Santa Barbara.

Green trough
of between mountains
through which a single
pigeon sails,

the hill-crest held
on the edge of its plunge
the wave
before it breaks down

and, in profile
against the curved green
breaker of forest

the ease-bringing
dove.

The Fist

The fist clenched round my heart
loosens a little, and I gasp
brightness; but it tightens
again. When have I ever not loved
the pain of love? But this has moved

past love to mania. This has the strong
clench of the madman, this is
gripping the ledge of unreason, before
plunging howling into the abyss.

Hold hard then, heart. This way at least you live.

Love After Love

The time will come
when, with elation,
you will greet yourself arriving
at your own door, in your own mirror,
and each will smile at the other's welcome,

and say sit here. Eat.
You will love again the stranger who was your self,
Give wine. Give bread. Give back your heart
to itself, to the stranger who has loved you

all your life, whom you ignored
for another, who knows you by heart.
Take down the love-letters from the bookshelf

the photographs, the desperate notes,
peel your own image from the mirror.
Sit. Feast on your life.

Midsummer, England

At Henley, the sky-blue striped pavilions
are boat-houses, the royal river
beer-bottle green with broken lights,
the legendary landscapes are alive,
palpable air; woods, castles, manors, suns,
pressing their postcards on you as you drive.

Great summer takes its ease,
ankling the shallows, cloudy dresses bloat
and cling clearly round the women's knees,
as Christ harangues the indifferent from his boat
by Cookham's river.

Riots of colour in the Supplements,
startling bright mustard squares
flare tropically up amid
fields trimmed by centuries of reticence;
midsummer's broad abandon will subside
like hills rolling in heat waves; what will not,
is the fear of darkness entering England's vein,
the noble monuments pissed on by rain,
the imperial blood corrupted, the dark tide.

But summer persists through the pain,
it forces the leaf
and tries, through love-nourishing rain
to dissolve individual grief,
history and heart-break.

Prodigious summer whose black fruit includes,
past this and that great house,
between hills bracketing thunder,
a great cloud's shadow that grows close
as the past, a chill that intrudes
under the heat, under the centuries;
rooks swinging in the wind, under great boughs,
lynched crows, on a green field.

What hurts most is to think that I was healed.

The Bright Field

My nerves steeled against the power of London,
I hurried home that evening, with the sense
we all have, of the crowd's hypocrisy,
to feel my rage, turned on in self-defence,
bear mercy for the anonymity
of every self humbled by massive places,
and I, who moved against a bitter sea,
was moved by the light on Underground-bound faces.

Their sun that would not set was going down
on their flushed faces, brickwork like a kiln,
on pillar-box bright buses between trees,
with the compassion of calendar art;
like walking sheaves of harvest, the quick crowd
thickened in separate blades of cane or wheat
from factories and office doors conveyed
to one end by the loud belt of the street.
And that end brings its sadness, going in
by Underground, by cab, by bullock-cart,
and lances us with punctual, maudlin
pity down lanes or cane-fields, till the heart,
seeing, like dark canes, the river-spires sharpen,
feels an involuntary bell begin
to toll for everything, even in London,
heart of our history, original sin.

The vision that brought Samuel Palmer peace,
that stoked Blake's fury at her furnaces,
flashes from doormen's buttons and the rocks

around Balandra. These slow belfry-strokes
cast in the pool of London, from which swallows
rise in wide rings, and from their bright field, rooks,
mark the same beat by which a pelican goes
across Salybia as the tide lowers.

Dark August

So much rain, so much life like the swollen sky
of this black August. My sister, the sun,
broods in her yellow room and won't come out.

Everything goes to hell; the mountains fume
like a kettle, rivers over-run, still,
she will not rise and turn off the rain.

She's in her room, fondling old things,
my poems, turning her album. Even if thunder falls
like a crash of plates from the sky,

she does not come out.
Don't you know I love you but am hopeless
at fixing the rain? But I am learning slowly

to love the dark days, the steaming hills,
the air with gossiping mosquitoes,
and to sip the medicine of bitterness,

so that when you emerge, my sister,
parting the beads of the rain,
with your forehead of flowers and eyes of forgiveness,

all will not be as it was, but it will be true,
(you see they will not let me love
as I want), because my sister, then

I would have learnt to love black days like bright ones,
the black rain, the white hills, when once
I loved only my happiness and you.

Sea Canes

Half my friends are dead.
I will make you new ones, said earth,
No, give me them back, as they were, instead
with faults and all, I cried.

Tonight I can snatch their talk
from the faint surf's drone,
through the canes, but I cannot walk

on the moonlit leaves of ocean
down that white road alone,
or float with the dreaming motion

of owls leaving earth's load.
O earth, the number of friends you keep
exceeds those left to be loved.

The sea-canes by the cliff flash green and silver
they were the seraph lances of my faith,
but out of what is lost grows something stronger

that has the rational radiance of stone,
enduring moonlight, further than despair,
strong as the wind, that through dividing canes

brings those we love before us, as they were,
with faults and all, not nobler, just there.

The Harvest

If they ask what my favourite flower was,
there's one thing that you'll have to understand:
I learnt to love it by the usual ways
of those who swore to serve truth with one hand,
and one behind their back for cash or praise,
that I surrendered dreaming how I'd stand
in the rewarding autumn of my life,
just ankle-deep in money, thick as leaves,
to bring my poetry, poor, faithful wife
past her accustomed style, well, all the same,
though there's no autumn, nature played the game
with me each fiscal year, when the gold pouis
would guiltily start scattering largesse
like Christian bankers or wind-shook-down thieves.
What I soon learnt was they had changed the script,
left out the golden fall and turned to winter,
to some grey monochrome, much like this metre,
with no gold in it. So, I saw my toil
as a seedy little yard of scrub and root
that gripped for good, and what took in that soil,
was the cheap flower that you see at my foot,
the coarsest, commonest, toughest, nondescript,
resilient violet with its white spot centre.

Midsummer, Tobago

Broad sun-stoned beaches.

White heat.
A green river.

A bridge,
scorched yellow palms

from the summer-sleeping house
drowsing through August.

Days I have held,
days I have lost,

days that outgrow, like daughters,
my harbouring arms.

Force

Life will keep hammering the grass blades into the ground.

I admire this violence;
love is iron. I admire

the brutal exchange between breaker and rock.
They have an understanding.

I may even understand the contract
between the galloping lion and the stunned doe,
there is some yes to terror in her eyes

what I will never understand
is the beast who writes this
and claims the centre of life.

Oddjob, a Bull Terrier

You prepare for one sorrow,
but another comes.
It is not like the weather,
you cannot brace yourself,
the unreadiness is all.
Your companion, the woman,
the friend next to you,
the child at your side,
and the dog,
we tremble for them,
we look sea-ward and muse
it will rain.
We shall get ready for rain,
you do not connect
the sunlight altering
the darkening oleanders
in the sea-garden,
the gold going out of the palms.
You do not connect this
the fleck of the drizzle
on your flesh
with the dog's whimper,
the thunder doesn't frighten,
the readiness is all,
what follows at your feet
is trying to tell you
the silence is all
it is deeper than the readiness,
it is sea-deep,

earth-deep,
love-deep.

The silence
is stronger than thunder,
we are stricken dumb and deep
as the animals who never utter love
as we do, except
it becomes unutterable
and must be said,
in a whimper,
in tears,
in the drizzle that comes to our eyes
not uttering the loved thing's name,
the silence of the dead,
the silence of the deepest buried love is
the one silence,
and whether we bear it for beast,
for child, for woman, or friend,
it is the one love, it is the same,
and it is blest
deepest by loss
it is blest, it is blest.

Earth

Let the day grow on you upward
through your feet
the vegetal knuckles

to your knees of stone,
until by evening you are a black tree;
feel, with evening,

the swifts thicken your hair,
the new moon rising out of your forehead,
and the moonlit veins of silver

running from your armpits
like rivulets under white leaves.
Sleep, as ants

cross over your eyelids.
You have never possessed anything
as deeply as this.

This is all you have owned
from the first outcry
through forever;

you can never be dispossessed.

At Last

To the exiled novelists

You spit on your people,
your people applaud,
your former oppressors
laurel you.
The thorns biting your forehead
are contempt
disguised as concern,
still, you can come home, now.
Before, in your finical gut
the bowels of compassion
petrify to a gallstone,
and your ink deliquesces
into bile. In your eye
every child is born crippled,
every endeavour
is that of the baboon,
can you hear the achievement
of this chimpanzee typing?

We are through with that pastoral
of palm-splashed zebras
soundlessly circling
nostalgic veldts,
with the caved-in balafong
and the snapped strings
of savannah grass,
let your fur-shrouded
Aryan horseman
melt into the snowstorm,

till the page is again
blank, and, under the snowdrift
of the white page, of the white
ocean, all is buried,
generations, generations.

The snows have hardened,
the page is cold, it is glazed
like the snow-lashed eyes
and the freaked, parted mouths
of your horsemen, like the dice
of skulls rolling under
the tilting sea-floor.
Generations, generations,
they did not cross for us to abhor
them, they did not all die
for your prose, those who
perished in the snows or
under the snow-torn billows,

nor do they need to forgive
their children who tear
at the scabs of their names.
We have passed through the fever,
when we heard our voices
when the bells of the anopheles
were ringing in the ears
over the rice-fields,
over the sea-canes
when the morning sunlight
shivered with malaria,
and the night sea grew tepid
with weeds, like a bush-bath.

We have sweated cold sweat
remembering generations,

while you, who have risen
from their sweat-soaked capra
from the tangled night-bed
folded over like snowdrifts
should know that the sun
is no longer ill,
an orange infested with ants,
that this landscape was never
forgiven or forgiving,
while the pelican beats
to the rock of Soledad
to a beat which is neither
poetry nor prose.

I have sweated it out,
generations, generations,
I am growing hoarse
from repeating the praise
of the ape and the ass,
the enslaved, the indentured,
who are nothing. Grass, then
dung. Paths for the good
to walk over. Men.

And now, let it come to fruit,
let me be sure it has flowered
to break from the bitterest root
and the earth that soured,
the flower bursts out of my heart,
the cleft in the rock, at last
flowers, the heart-breaking past
unforgiven and unforgiving,
the net of my veins I have cast
here flashes with living
silver at last, at last!

Winding Up

I live on the water,
alone. Without wife and children.
I have circled every possibility
to come to this:

a low house by grey water,
with windows always open
to the stale sea. We do not choose such things,

but we are what we have made.
We suffer, the years pass,
we shed freight but not our need

for encumbrances. Love is a stone
that settled on the sea-bed
under grey water. Now, I require nothing

from poetry, but true feeling,
no pity, no fame, no healing. Silent wife,
we can sit watching grey water,

and in a life awash
with mediocrity and trash
live rock-like.

I shall unlearn feeling,
unlearn my gift. That is greater
and harder than what passes there for life.

The Morning Moon

Still haunted by the cycle of the moon
racing full sail
past the crouched whale's back of Morne Coco mountain,

I gasp at her sane brightness.

It's early December,
the breeze freshens the skin of this earth,
the goose-skin of water,

and I notice the blue plunge
of shadows down Morne Coco mountain,
December's sun-dial,

happy that the earth is still changing
that the full moon can blind me with her forehead
this bright foreday morning,

and that fine sprigs of white are springing from my beard.

To Return to the Trees

for John Figueroa

Senex, an oak.
Senex, this old sea-almond
unwincing in spray

in this geriatric grove
on the sea-road to Cumana.
To return to the trees,

to decline like this tree,
the burly oak
of Boanerges Ben Jonson!

Or, am I lying
like this felled almond
when I write I look forward to age

a gnarled poet
bearded with the whirlwind,
his metres like thunder?

It is not only the sea,
no, for on windy, green mornings
I read the changes on Morne Coco Mountain,

from flagrant sunrise
to its ashen end;
grey has grown strong to me,

it's no longer neutral,
no longer the dirty flag
of courage going under,

it is speckled with hues
like quartz, it's as
various as boredom,

grey now is a crystal
haze, a dull diamond,
stone-dusted and stoic,

grey is the heart at peace,
tougher than the warrior
as it bestrides factions,

it is the great pause
when the pillars of the temple
rest on Samson's palms

and are held, held,
that moment
when the heavy rock of the world

like a child sleeps
on the trembling shoulders of Atlas
and his own eyes close,

the toil that is balance.
Seneca, that fabled bore,
and his gnarled, laborious Latin

I can read only in fragments
of broken bark, his
heroes tempered by whirlwinds,

who see with the word
senex, with its two eyes,
through the boles of this tree,

beyond joy,
beyond lyrical utterance,
this obdurate almond

going under the sand
with this language, slowly,
by sand grains, by centuries.